THE MINDFULNESS IN PLAIN ENGLISH

Journal

THE
MINDFULNESS
IN PLAIN ENGLISH

Journal

WITH MEDITATION INSTRUCTIONS FROM
Bhante Gunaratana

A NOTE ABOUT THIS JOURNAL

This journal, like the practice of mindfulness, is about your life. What you'll find from me in these pages is, first, a brief introduction to mindfulness for beginners—and in a real way, with mindfulness we're all beginners! Throughout the rest of the journal I share some tips, encouragements, and gentle reminders that I hope might be helpful to you. Though I've offered a few words here, the most important part of this book will be what *you* do with it.

You might use this journal to reflect on the ways you are bringing mindfulness into your life—what you are learning and where you struggle, and the big and little ways all those things change. You might use this space to express specific mindful intentions for each day or to keep track of your mindful explorations. Or you might use the mindfulness teachings as prompts for mini-meditations—and do a few minutes of practice before you dive into wherever your creativity takes you.

It's your journal, your life, and your practice—may it serve you well!

—Bhante G.

THE PRACTICE OF
Mindfulness

S IT UPRIGHT and allow your body to become motionless, completely still. After sitting motionlessly, close your eyes. Our mind is analogous to a cup of muddy water. The longer you keep a cup of muddy water still, the more the mud settles down and the water will be seen clearly. Similarly, if you keep quiet without moving your body, focusing your entire undivided attention on the subject of your meditation, your mind settles down and begins to experience the fruits of meditation.

We should keep our mind in the present moment. Every moment is a moment of events and no moment passes by without an event. We cannot notice a moment without noticing events taking place in that moment. Therefore, the moment we try to pay bare attention to is the present moment. Our mind goes through a series of events like a series of pictures passing through a projector. Some of these pictures are coming from our past experiences and others are our imaginations of things that we plan to do in the future.

The mind can never be focused without a mental object. Therefore we must give our mind an object that is readily available every present moment. One such object is our breath. The mind does not have to make a great effort to find the breath. Every moment the breath is flowing in and out through our nostrils. As our practice of insight meditation is taking place every waking moment, our mind finds it very easy to focus itself on the breath, for it is more conspicuous and constant than any other object.

To begin, take three deep breaths. After taking three deep breaths, breathe normally, letting your breath flow in and out freely, effortlessly, and begin focusing your attention on the rims of your nostrils. Simply notice the feeling of breath going in and out. When one inhalation is complete and before exhaling begins, there is a brief pause. Notice it and notice the beginning of exhaling. When the exhalation is complete, there is another brief pause before inhaling begins. Notice this brief pause, too. This means that there are two brief pauses of breath—one at the end of inhaling and the other at the end of exhaling. These two pauses occur in such a brief moment you may not be aware of their occurrence. But when you are mindful, you can notice them.

Do not verbalize or conceptualize anything. Simply notice the incoming and outgoing breath without saying, "I breathe in," or "I breathe out." When you focus your attention on the breath, ignore any thought, memory, sound, smell, taste, etc., and focus your attention exclusively on the breath, nothing else.

At the beginning, both the inhalations and exhalations are short because the body and mind are not calm and relaxed. Notice the feeling of that short inhaling and short exhaling as they occur without saying, "short inhaling," or "short exhaling." As you continue to notice the feeling of short inhaling and short exhaling, your body and mind become relatively calm. Then your breath becomes long. Notice the feeling of that long breath as it is without saying, "Long breath." Then notice the entire breathing process from the beginning to the end. Subsequently the breath becomes subtle, and the mind and body become calmer than before. Notice this calm and peaceful feeling of your breathing.

Mindfulness Tip

DON'T EXPECT ANYTHING. Just sit back and see what happens. Treat the whole thing as an experiment. Take an active interest in the test itself, but don't get distracted by your expectations about the results. For that matter, don't be anxious for any result whatsoever. Let the meditation move along at its own speed and in its own direction. Let the meditation teach you. Meditative awareness seeks to see reality exactly as it is. Whether that corresponds to our expectations or not, it does require a temporary suspension of all of our preconceptions and ideas. We must store our images, opinions, and interpretations out of the way for the duration of the session. Otherwise we will stumble over them.

....

....

....

....

....

....

....

....

....

....

....

....

....

....

....

....

Mindfulness is a lovely way to perceive the world,
and it is a learnable skill.

Open your eyes and the world pours in . . .

. . . blink and it is gone.

The present moment is changing so fast . . .

. . . that we often do not notice its existence at all.

According to the Buddha, our minds are naturally luminous.

You can only have bliss if you don't chase it.

Mindfulness Tip

DISCOMFORT IN MEDITATION is an opportunity. When you see a truck bearing down on you, by all means jump out of the way. But spend some time in meditation too, and learn to work with discomfort. Learning to deal with discomfort is the only way you'll be ready to handle the truck you didn't see.

Your own practice can show you the truth.

....

....

....

....

....

....

....

....

....

....

....

....

....

....

....

....

Your own experience is all that counts.

Nothing worthwhile is achieved overnight.

The you that goes in
one side of the meditation experience . . .

. . . is not the same you that comes out the other side.

Change, change, change;
no two moments are ever the same.

Perpetual fluctuation is the nature of the universe.

Don't strain.
Don't force anything or make grand, exaggerated efforts.

Just let your effort be relaxed and steady.

It is said that there are only two tragedies in life:

not getting what one wants—and getting it.

If you pursue pleasure, you'll also find pain . . .

. . . both come together in one package.

Mindfulness Tip

DON'T RUSH. There is no hurry, so take your time. Settle yourself on a cushion and sit as though you have the whole day. Anything really valuable takes time to develop. Patience, patience, patience.

There is no pleasure without some degree of pain.

There is no pain without some amount of pleasure.

If you really look carefully . . .

. . . you'll discover no moment is ever boring.

Let come what comes . . .

. . . and accommodate yourself
to all that you meet, whatever it is.

The more flexible you are with your mindfulness practice . . .

. . . the more useful it will be.

Let go of the habit
of clinging to people and things . . .

. . . and let go of the habit
of clinging to ideas, beliefs, and opinions.

Mindfulness Tip

DON'T CLING TO ANYTHING, AND DON'T REJECT ANYTHING. Let come what comes, and accommodate yourself to that, whatever it is. If good mental images arise, that is fine. If bad mental images arise, that is fine, too. Look on all of it as equal, and make yourself comfortable with whatever happens. Don't fight with what you experience, just observe it all mindfully.

Don't think. *See.*

Pain is inevitable . . .

. . . suffering is not.

Blaming the world for your discontent . . .

. . . keeps you mired in unhappiness.

The moment you accept responsibility for your situation . . .

. . . you begin to move in a positive direction.

The essence of our experience is change.

Change is incessant.

Mindfulness Tip

LET GO. There is no need to freeze time and no need to grasp on to experience. There is no need to block things out and no need to ignore them. Learn to flow with all the changes that come up. Loosen up and relax.

Moment by moment life flows by . . .

. . . and moment by moment it changes.

Let go, loosen up, and relax.

Whatever attitudes we habitually use toward ourselves . . .

. . . we will use on others.

Whatever attitudes we habitually use toward others . . .

. . . we will use on ourselves.

You can't ever get everything you want—
luckily, there is another option:

You can learn to work with your mind.

Meditation is running into reality.

Mindfulness Tip

ACCEPT EVERYTHING THAT ARISES. Accept your feelings, even the ones you wish you did not have. Accept your experiences, even the ones you hate. Don't condemn yourself for having human flaws and failings. Learn to see all the phenomena in the mind as being perfectly natural and understandable. Try to exercise a disinterested acceptance at all times with respect to everything you experience.

Mindfulness allows you to delve deeply into life.

Accept everything that arises.

Accept your feelings . . .

. . . even the ones you wish you did not have.

Accept your experiences . . .

. . . even the ones you hate.

Don't condemn yourself
for being human and having human flaws.

Mindfulness Tip

BE GENTLE WITH YOURSELF. Be kind to yourself. You may not be perfect, but you are all you've got to work with. The process of becoming who you will be begins first with the total acceptance of who you are.

Learn to see all the phenomena in the mind . . .

. . . as being perfectly natural and understandable.

Let come whatever comes.

Let go whatever goes.

There is a difference between watching the mind . . .

. . . and *controlling* the mind.

Watching the mind with a gentle, open attitude . . .

. . . allows the mind to settle down and come to rest.

Trying to control the mind . . .

. . . just stirs up more agitation and suffering.

Mindfulness Tip

INVESTIGATE YOURSELF. Question everything. Take nothing for granted. Don't believe anything because it sounds wise and pious and some holy man said it. See for yourself. That does not mean that you should be cynical, impudent, or irreverent—it means you should be *empirical*. Subject all statements to the actual test of your own experience, and let the results be your guide to truth. Insight meditation evolves out of an inner longing to wake up to what is real and to gain liberating insight into the true structure of existence. The entire practice hinges upon this desire to be awake to the truth. Without it, the practice is superficial.

Meditation is participatory observation.

What you are looking at
responds to the process of looking.

What you are looking at is *you*.

What you see depends on how you look.

Be gentle with yourself.

Be kind to yourself.

You may not be perfect . . .

. . . but you are all you've got to work with.

Mindfulness Tip

VIEW ALL PROBLEMS AS CHALLENGES. Just because of the simple fact that you are human, you find yourself heir to a certain inherent unsatisfactoriness in life that simply will not go away. Look upon difficulties that arise as opportunities to learn and to grow. Don't run from them, condemn yourself, or bury your burden in saintly silence. You have a problem? Great. More grist for the mill. Rejoice, dive in, and investigate.

The process of becoming who you will be . . .

. . . begins first with the total acceptance of who you are.

Ignorance may be bliss . . .

. . . but it does not lead to liberation.

Investigate yourself.

Question everything.

Take nothing for granted.

Mindfulness Tip

DON'T PONDER. You don't need to figure everything out. Discursive thinking won't free you from the trap. In meditation, the mind is purified naturally by mindfulness, by wordless bare attention. Habitual deliberation is not necessary to eliminate those things that are keeping you in bondage. All that is necessary is a clear, nonconceptual perception of what they are and how they work. That alone is sufficient to dissolve them. Concepts and reasoning just get in the way.

Don't believe anything because it sounds wise.

See for yourself.

Moment-to-moment mindfulness
helps you avoid regrettable actions.

The way out of a trap is to study the trap itself . . .

. . . and learn how it is built.

Whatever problem is before you,
try viewing it as a challenge.

The practice of mindfulness
is something you can do anywhere, anytime.

Mindfulness Tip

DON'T DWELL UPON CONTRASTS. **Differences** do exist between people, but dwelling upon them is a dangerous process. Unless carefully handled, this leads directly to egotism. Ordinary human thinking is full of greed, jealousy, and pride. A man seeing another man on the street may immediately think, "He is better looking than I am." The instant result is envy or shame. A girl seeing another girl may think, "I am prettier than she is." The instant result is pride. This sort of comparison is a mental habit, and it leads directly to ill feeling of one sort or another. It is an unskillful mental state, but we do it all the time. We compare our looks with others, our success, accomplishments, wealth, possessions, or IQ, and all of this leads to the same state—estrangement, barriers between people, and ill feeling.

Rejoice, dive in, and investigate.

Dive in, investigate, and rejoice.

....

....

....

....

....

....

....

....

....

....

....

....

....

....

....

....

Meditation takes gumption.

When you are having a bad time,
examine that badness . . .

. . . observe it mindfully,
study the phenomenon, learn its mechanics.

Use your speech wisely.

Avoid overindulgence.

Mindfulness Tip

PRACTICE SKILLFUL SPEECH. Skillful speech not only means that we pay attention to the words we speak and to their tone but also requires that our words reflect compassion and concern for others and that they help and heal, rather than wound and destroy.

Remember to strive for peace with those around you.

Close your eyes for just one minute
and you can experience . . .

. . . how a feeling or emotion is born,
grows old, and passes away.

Everything is permanently impermanent.

Mindfulness Tip

DON'T STRAIN. Don't force anything or make grand, exaggerated efforts. Meditation is not aggressive. There is no place or need for violent striving. Just let your effort be relaxed and steady.

The Dharma is shelter we can always rely on . . .

. . . if we simply remember to.

Wisdom Publications
199 Elm Street
Somerville, MA 02144 USA
wisdompubs.org

Library of Congress Cataloging-in-Publication Data is available.

ISBN 978-1-61429-396-5

20 19 18 17 16
5 4 3 2 1

Cover and interior design by Gopa&Ted2, Inc.
Set in Guardi LT Std 10/16.5 and MrsEaves 13/16.

Wisdom Publications' books are printed on acid-free paper and meet
the guidelines for permanence and durability of the Production Guidelines for Book Longevity of the Council on Library Resources.

❀ This book was produced with environmental mindfulness.
For more information, please visit wisdompubs.org/wisdom-environment.

Printed in the PRC.

About Wisdom Publications

Wisdom Publications is the leading publisher of classic and contemporary Buddhist books and practical works on mindfulness. To learn more about us or to explore our other books, please visit our website at wisdompubs.org or contact us at the address below.

Wisdom Publications
199 Elm Street
Somerville, MA 02144 USA

We are a 501(c)(3) organization, and donations in support of our mission are tax deductible.

Wisdom Publications is affiliated with the Foundation for the Preservation of the Mahayana Tradition (FPMT).